Being sexy is all about attitude, not body type. It's a state of mind.

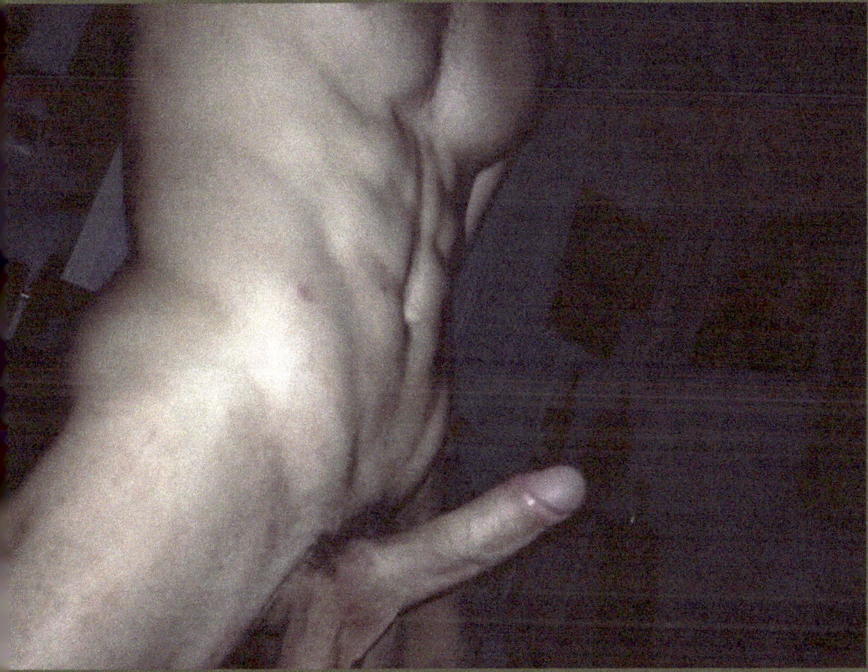

orona
xtra

ripcurl
PINS

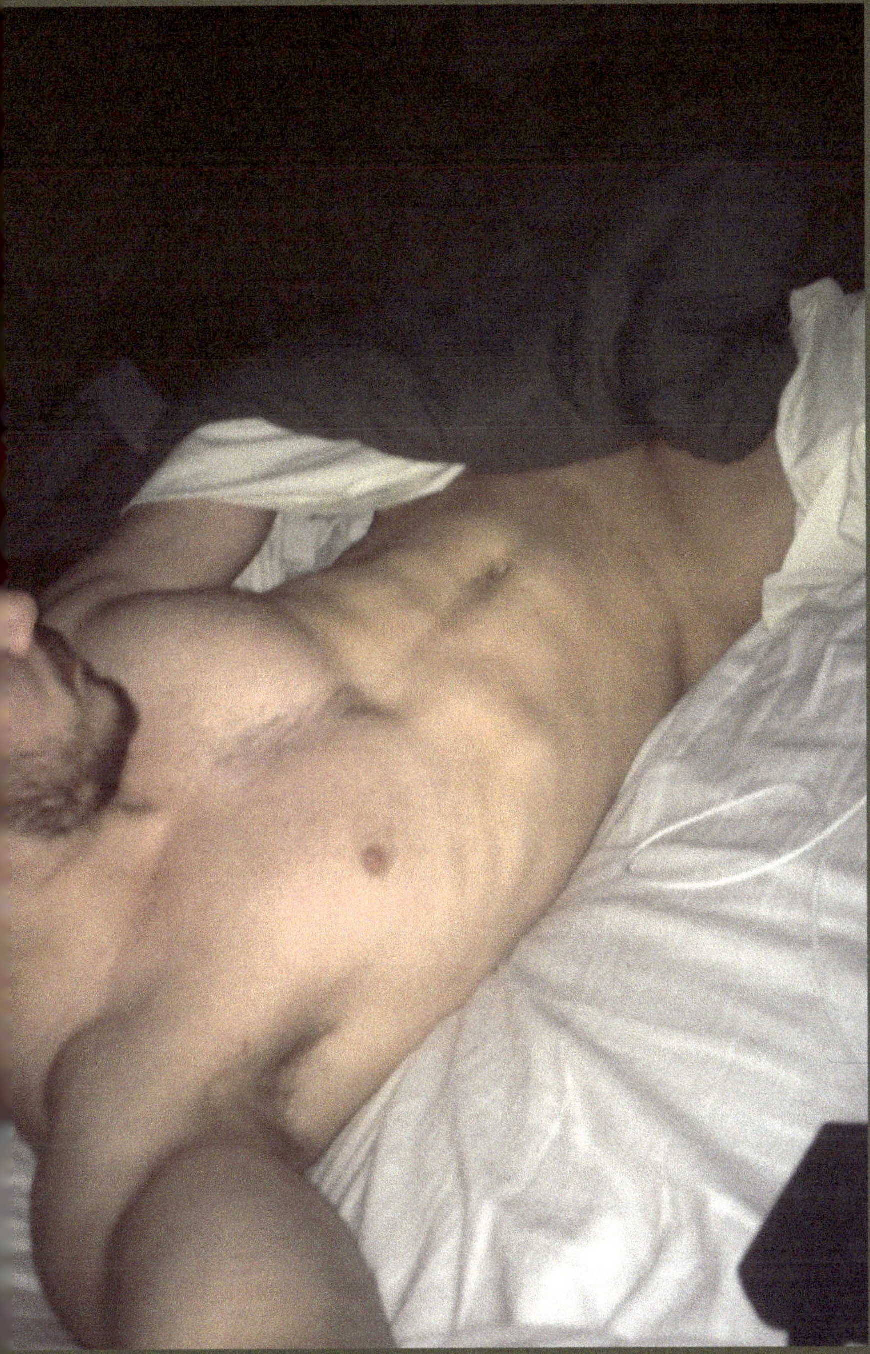

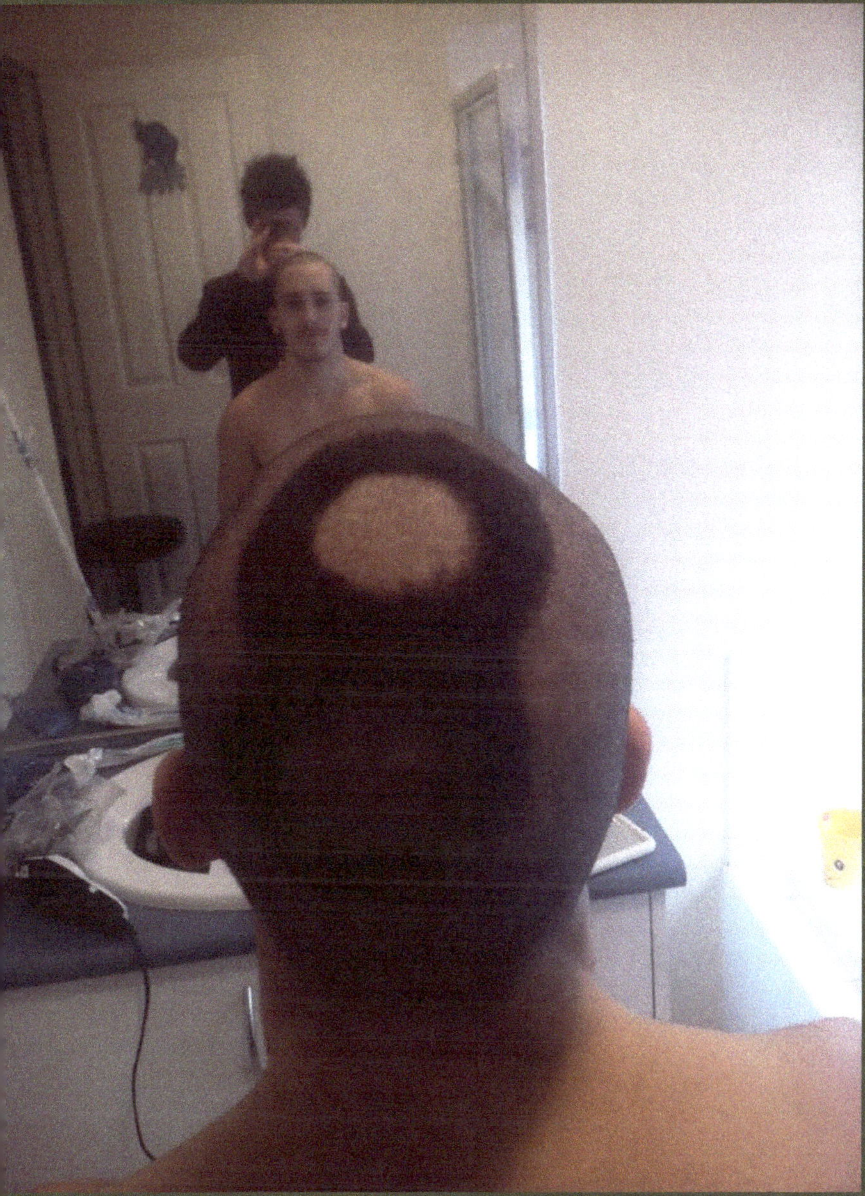

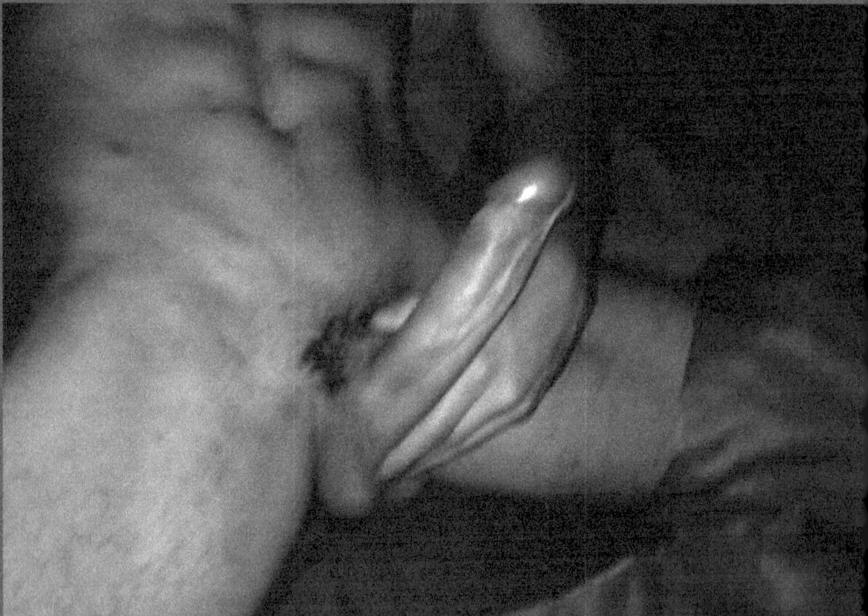

Klein

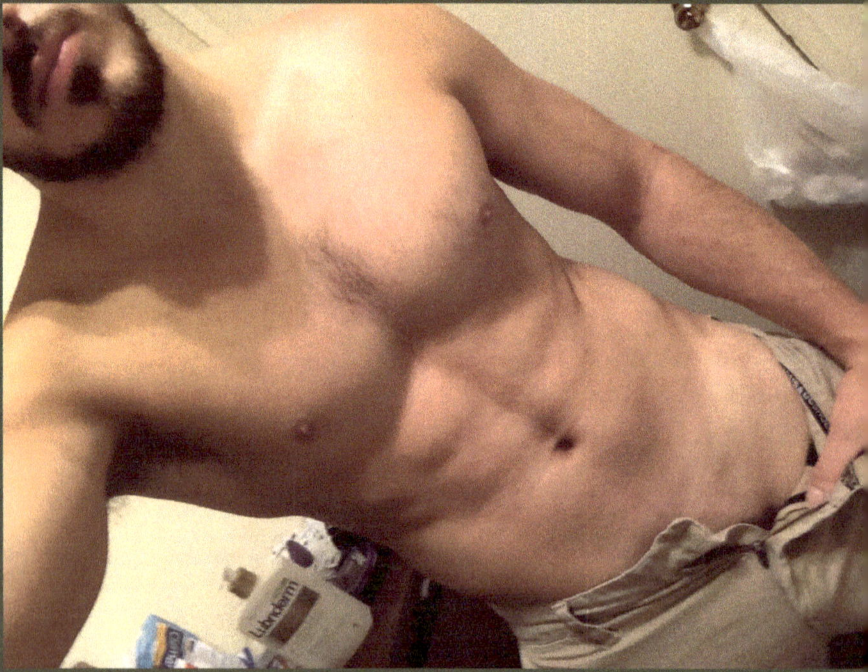

Lubriderm

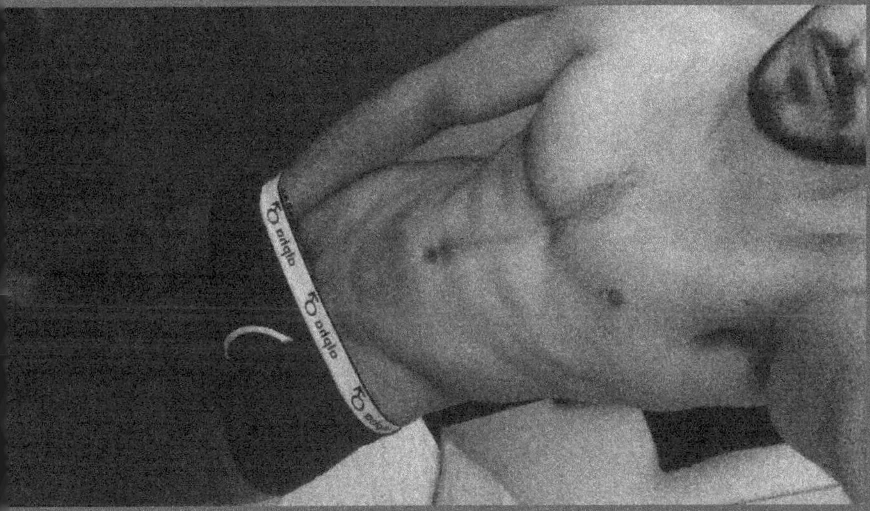

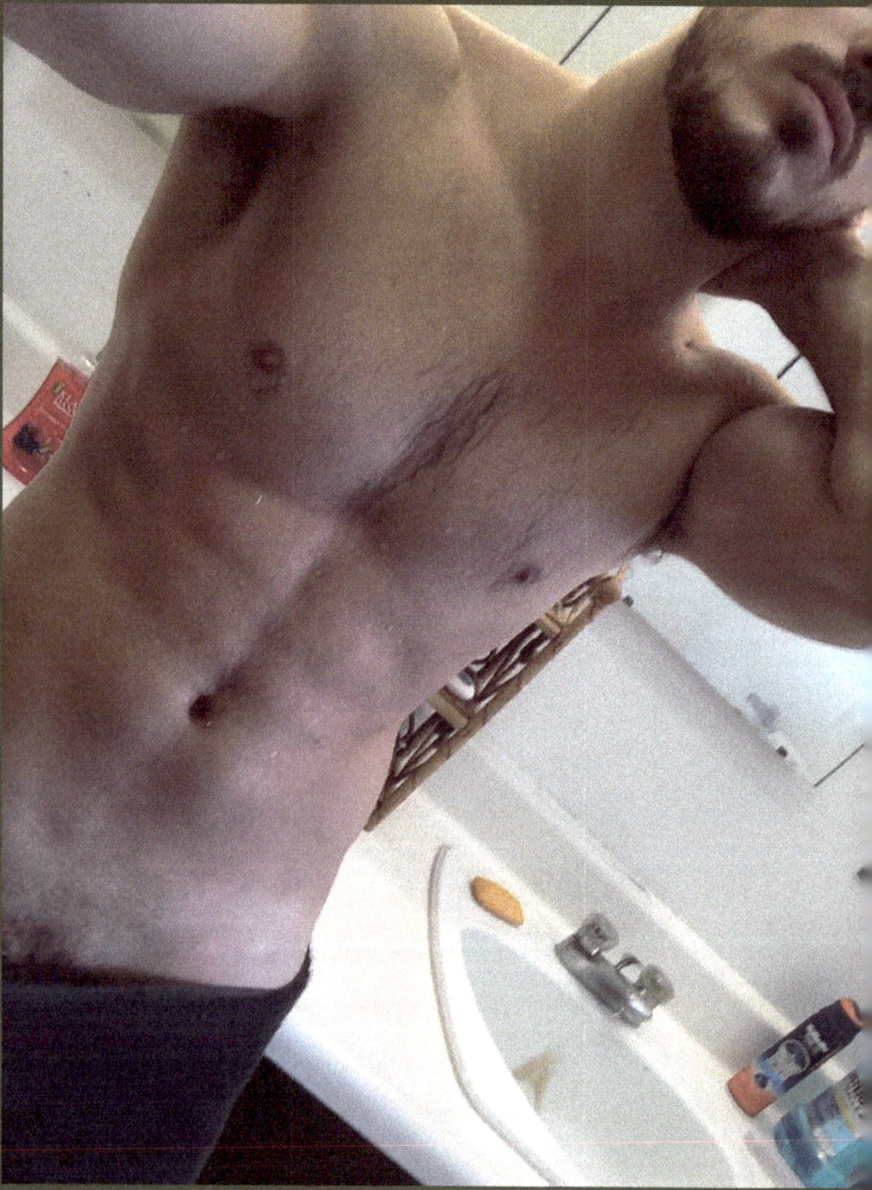

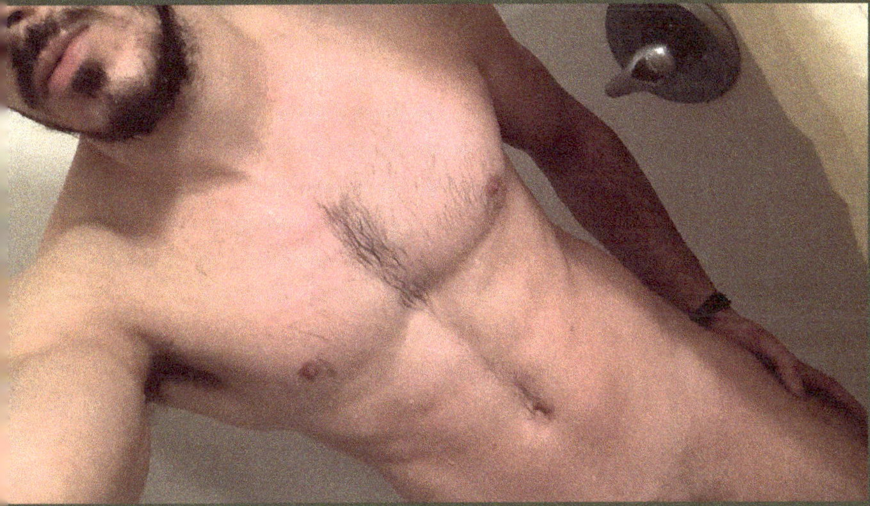

MIX
MIX

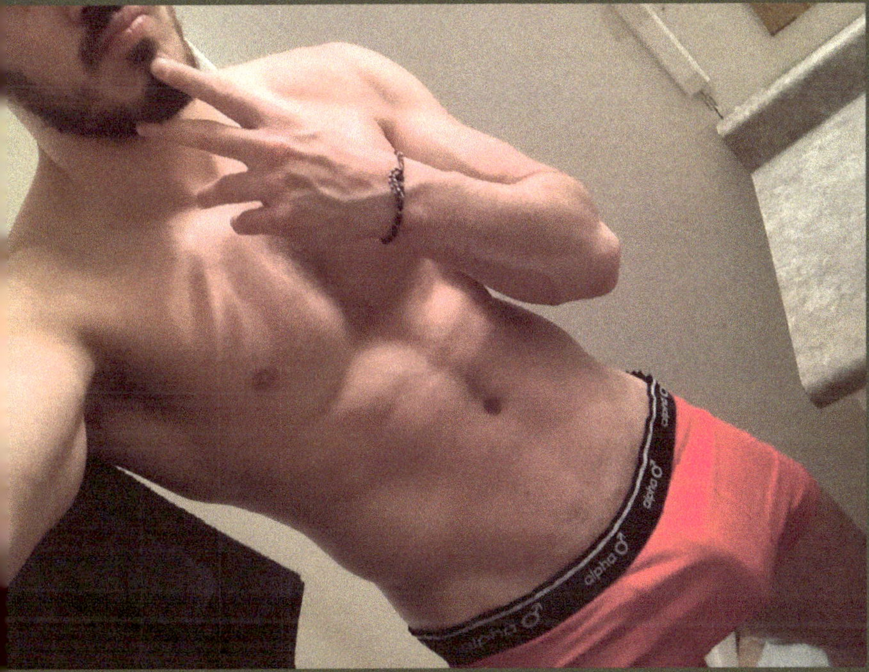

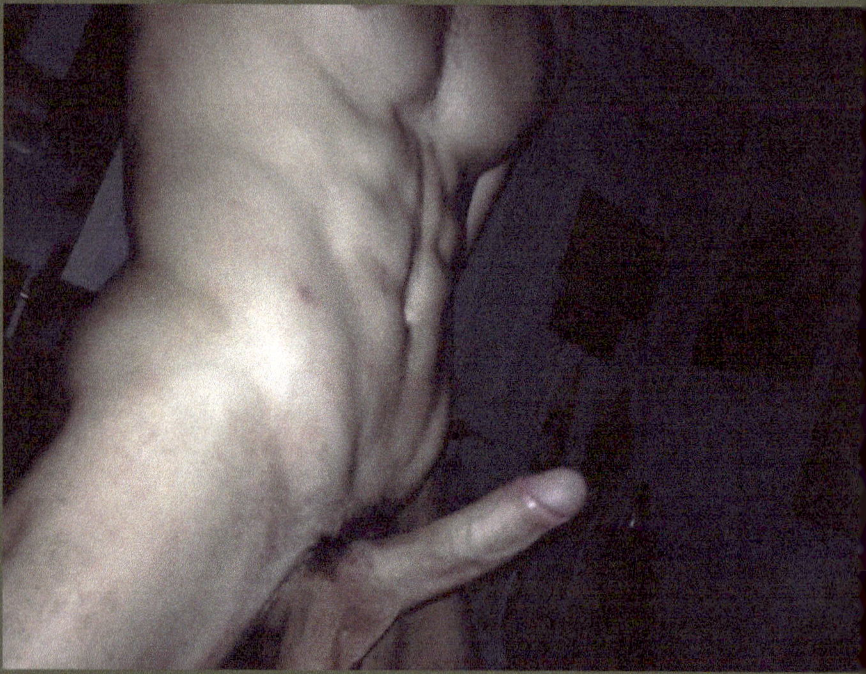

CPSIA information can be obtained
at www.ICGtesting.com
Printed in the USA
BVHW021220150319
542770BV00013B/105/P

9 780368 405358